Half

Half Way to Madrid

NADINE BRUMMER

All rights reserved. No part of this work covered by the copyright hereon may be reproduced or used in any form by any means – graphic, electronic, or mechanical, including copying, recording, taping, or information storage and retrieval systems – without written permission of the publisher.

Typeset and Printed by Q3 Print Project Management Ltd, Loughborough (01509 213456)

Published by Shoestring Press
19 Devonshire Avenue, Beeston, Nottingham, NG9 1BS
Telephone: (0115) 925 1827
www.shoestringpress.co.uk

First published 2002
© Copyright: Nadine Brummer
ISBN: 1 899549 70 6

Shoestring Press gratefully acknowledges financial assistance from East Midlands Arts

Acknowledgements

Some of the poems included in HALF WAY TO MADRID first appeared in the following publications: *European Judaism, Lines Review, London Magazine, New Blackfriars, Other Poetry, Poetry London, Poetry Wales, the Rialto, Staple, Writing Women.* "That Rank Bed" and "Why is This Night Different from All Other Nights" were published in the anthology, PARENTS, Enitharmon Press, 2000, and "At The Lucian Freud Exhibition" was published in the anthology Dybbuk of Delight, Five Leaves Press. Twenty of the poems, sometimes in slightly different versions, were published in A QUESTION OF BLUE TULIPS AND OTHER POEMS, Shoestring Press, 1999.

I owe much to mentors and friends and especially to Pat de Maré.

to Margaret Richards

Contents

At The Lucian Freud Exhibition	1
Torn	3
That Rank Bed	4
I'm Still Interrogating My Sister	5
"Why Is This Night Different From All Other Nights?"	6
Great Uncle Velve	8
'Und Sonst Garnichts' (May 1992)	9
Between Two Lives	10
A Question of Blue Tulips	12
Black Fruits	14
Wild Women's Week-End?	15
The Kaleidoscope	17
Rent	19
House	20
The Visit	21
The Hill	22
Margaret's House	23
Through a Door in a Wall	24
The Frog's Princess	26
Face-To-Face	27
Ferret	28
The Cat Who Is Game For Anything	29
Out Of Summer	30
White	31
Half Way To Madrid	32
Tailors	33
Further On	34
"When Epiphany Occurred And You Met The God"	35
The Eye-Bath	36
Photographer	37
Monk of Hemis, Ladakh	38
The Copper Beech	40
Foxgloves	41
Blackthorn	42
Larva	43
Snailing	44
Snow Globe	45
Homing In	46
Cactus	47
The Game	48

Glasses	49
Skins	50
First Nation Masks	51
Mask	52
Hazel Nuts	53
Danäe Compares Notes With Europa	54
The Back-yard Tree	55
The Buzzard	56
Curtains	57
Eryngium	58
Frescoes	59
Blvd. Montmartre: after Pissarro	60
Minoans	61
In My Aunt's Bedroom	62
Thuja Tree	63
Pollard	65
No Time To Reflect	66
The Cultivator of Silkworms Questions The Oracle	68

AT THE LUCIAN FREUD EXHIBITION

Head, hands, genitals and feet
are main events – he does them well.
Excess between is flesh, like meat.

And even now it takes some nerve to look
at turkey gizzards limp between men's legs
and women opening to a swarm of black.

Oh there's a buzz all right. Once at another show
I heard a woman in a hat enthuse
about a clever orchid, how

lips form a helipad for flies
which land in ruts, are trapped then sucked
where male and female parts are fused,

though none are needed for the helleborine
quite self-sufficient with its seed.
Can flowers be both gorgeous and obscene?

Leigh Bowery's back is overgrown with flecks,
an orchidaceous pink, buttocks sag
into an off-white stool. You sense the cracks

of old enamel bowls and chipped chrome taps
behind a drape. In front a red-brown rug
bristles. These genteel props

touch my eyes. Below each covering a frame,
upholding surfaces of this and that,
lies coiled, and I am forced to look again

at how I live. This cold October day
I'm in a crowd well heeled and buttoned up
engrossed with such carnality

I fear our coats might flake and tear
and eyes, preoccupied with doubt,
find bodies we'd not bargained for.

TORN

After my mother's death I found a cache
of old photos. One, torn in two, cuts off
my father's companion. He sports a tache,
looks handsome in khaki. The missing half?
I have the whole picture, can re-instate
the other woman. I remember when
Dad, on his first day's leave, sauntered in late
to a dried-up chicken breast and pan
of burnt latkas. My mother, distraught,
pummelled his chest. *He should have been here
where he belonged with his wife, he'd no right
to be there, drinking. Now the Shabbas dinner
was spoiled.* And the edge of her tongue was rough
as this photo's jag, where grandma's torn off.

THAT RANK BED

That rank bed,
my father only made lance-corporal.
Winceyette sheets,
my mother said sex hurts.
Why did I seek a place between
their humps of back-to-back
those childish half-clothed mornings?

He was hirsute,
she would not wear his hairiness,
she fitted her hernia behind a rosy belt.
Coils of thick pink piping,
some strange baby-cord,
dangled around holes
where babies start as lumps.

Wedlocked they worked
a double bed,
a loveless garden
where vows had gone to seed.
The child I was
still runs from the cold hours
to squeeze between them.

That rank breath,
the smell of fetid flowers
require some rare conception
some orchidaceous thing.
Over and over I try
to unearth an aestuous stem
to heal heartlands
laid waste in winceyette,
to salvage them.

I'M STILL INTERROGATING MY SISTER

Why are you the only child in the class
with clasped hands that seem to be saying
'please don't'? Thirty five others
have hands by their sides.
I suppose I was asleep in my cot
when that picture was taken.
You, in your grave, can't answer me back.
'It's alright', I still want to say,
'nothing too awful will happen'.
There's a newspaper shot of a boy
with his hands up, a helmet and gun
behind his peaked cap.
The brick wall of Temple School
wasn't the Warsaw Ghetto –
you were not being rounded up
so why were you standing like that?
Maybe, a minute before
you'd broken the no-talking rule
and teacher threatened to leave you out.
Of course you were not rehearsing
for when we were both grown up
and I, visiting your ward,
couldn't cope with your pleading.

"WHY IS THIS NIGHT DIFFERENT FROM ALL OTHER
NIGHTS?" ("MA NISHTANA ......?")

When there's a hint of spring, and the first crocus
begins its small festival, return
to catch a whiff of smoke at the kitchen door.

Observe the flames from silver candlesticks
how one is steady but another shivers
round a curled wick and may have to be snuffed.

Check the green dish with its small compartments
for parsley, shank bone and puttybrown paste
from nuts and wine. You're twelve in the country
of metaphor; as the youngest present recite
the 'Ma Nishtana' to begin the story.

Now admire your father who's decided to sing
like Gigli. Dip your finger in wine
to spatter ten drops on a plate, one at a time
and intone after him the ten plagues.

You may pull the tab in the blue Haggada.
Open the windows, one at a time, on the frogs,
the spotted people, the sheep upside down.
Was there a scene of blood on doorposts?
Recall the Egyptian children. Now reflect

on the room, how it's scrubbed and swept clean
of the last Hovis crumb. It's time for the meal,
so break a matzah in two and crush a hardboiled egg
into saltwater prepared by your father.

Can't you hear, as always, your mother nag
there's much too much salt?
Watch your father go red and the vein in his forehead throb.

But don't rush out the door because the night
isn't that different. Piece together the scene
in the cut glass of a decanter. Taste the cement's
richness – re-work a wall from wine and almonds.

And write a new story:
your parents sit bowed in the sand, wearied
by pyramids toppling over and the hauling
of slabs for pharaohs. Pretend
that you're Moses, the child they expected.

Take hold of their hands, his where dark hair
sprouts at his wrists, hers where the knuckles are rubbed
by a dishwater sea. Don't stay where you don't belong –
take them out of your childhood

to the land everyone's promised.
Leave them in peace, and stay at the border yourself
feeding off manna.

GREAT UNCLE VELVE

Great Uncle Velve chose to stay where he was,
fiddling in the shtetl.
No go-getter, he liked grass and poppy petals,
the way the men danced whitely at New Moon
bearding her with blessings, especially in summer
when unearthly vapour rose from hayfields
in swirls like prayer shawls.

'Nu go to New York', he cried to his brother
who wanted to skyscrape a living but made
only Manchester. Zayde wore a tape measure
round his neck like a phylactery strap,
sucked lemon tea over a sugar cube,
and didn't see the moon for fog and factory stacks,
but mainly because he stopped looking.
Who looks at the moon with thirteen mouths to feed?
– Only a schnorrer.

Great Uncle Velve in a village near Vitebsk,
preoccupied with God and an exuberant cow called Bashke,
ignored rumours of marching goyim but replied
occasionally to letters from his eldest nephew
who remembered, when he was four, how Uncle Velve
gave him spongecake dunked in vodka and he saw
a cockerel in baggy pantaloons. My uncle's accent
did not travel well but stayed
broken his whole life through.

Great Uncle Velve is for me a name
like velvet, a texture which
the sweatshops didn't know as well
as scrolls of law, bedded in their safe ark,
or those old fashioned curtains which closed out the dark
before they burned to ashes in the war.

'UND SONST GARNICHTS' (MAY 1992)

Dietrich is dead, frail, old, lame.
No elegies required to drag their feet
for cheekbones curved like the quick of the mind,
that his/her voice with its Germanic burr.

There are desires screened so darkly, yours,
mine, which basked in her like sharks
she'd tamed masterfully. Recall
her black hat tilted like a tall story.

To have been suave in loving, textured
for different sexual weathers – pure horn
of plenty! I see that now. It's early May,
cloud holds its cry of husky blue

breathtakingly. The first tender of copper beech
is such a passionate transaction – perhaps I'll weep.
I have this one life only
and it is burning a hole in my pocket.

Erotic God, ineffable Names of Lust,
let me not stay behind closed eyes in Spring.
World is sheer silk, body a corny thing
whose filmy visions and whose fantasies –

those little führers cracking dapper whips –
stalked fleapits full of men in sallow macs,
and women under lamps possessed
by light that's lost and always somewhere else.

I fear old age but hope it's spirited.
Hunger's a hole that fills the seven seas;
I'm falling in love again with everything there is,
where else is there to fall? Und sonst garnichts.

*'Und sonst garnichts' ('Apart from that, nothing') is the refrain of
Dietrich's famous song 'Falling in love again'*

BETWEEN TWO LIVES

Last week a fox,
stockstill on the lawn,
gazed with an effrontery
I envied, then loped away,
a creature between two lives.

My heart leapt up,
as it remembers to do
since school when colours shine
one at a time
as well as in rainbows.

One day I stood on the desk
for a dare, as high
as the top of the blackboard.
All class eight followed suit
staring Miss Hope in the eye.
We were sent for the strap.

In the rest of my life
I have not measured up
to that manifest gesture.

That fox had no right
to be on my patch
but I liked him there,
his hint of the wild–

the Cattistock hunt,
the scent of gorse, the musk
in an old badger hole

he, or a creature like him, found
to go to ground in.

Odd I most regret
sins I didn't commit
that were ruthless and bold –
the flaring of nostrils,
caps, whips and hipflasks.

My Hampstead fox
scavenges dustbins.

A QUESTION OF BLUE TULIPS

Blue tulips on a stall,
leaves dark-tipped
with dripped mascara ...

Once I saw Sarah Bellott
with a shock of bright green hair
stand on the doorstep
complaining of a red that hadn't worked.

She gave herself to being seen
that day. But why she stayed inside
so much with her unmarried brother,
nobody answered me that.

And no one spoke at all of Abey Zack,
braked across the street in his big chair.

I'd yell 'hello', then run
the risk of grunts, the choke
that started up his throat
and stopped his jaw. Don't stare.

Ignore him? How could I not greet
someone dressed for the fresh air
in his father's flat cap with a peak,
and a tartan rug over his knees,
winter and summer?

He'd watch me on my jaunt to school.
Nine-thirty prayers, then sums, then milk,
hands up for answers, heads on desks
for stories to be told, or sleep.
And there was learning by heart –

Abey and Sarah – items that stick.
The mind flips over, now and then,
missing bits: accidents
one might have wished unhappened.
Blue tulips? I prefer
red or yellow.

I change the colour of my hair,
and remember.

BLACK FRUITS

On my birthday I pick
black fruits that the sun
has brought to perfection.

It takes time to prefer
the gravity of sloes
to an orchard of apples –

that stony look where
a fluorescent blue
grows opaque.

The year on the turn
burns the air bright
with globules of black,

not glossy like wings
of a raven or hearse
but signs of a kingdom

buried and berried.
Demeter, perhaps,
laughed as she picked

fat fruits on thorns,
love-gifts exhumed
from her lost daughter.

WILD WOMEN'S WEEK-END?

"Come and find your power animal": the words
leap from yellow paper. Twined snakes, eyes
with purple irises are done in glitter paint.
The pamphlet names the Sacred Sweat Lodge
and items to bring, bangles and scarves,
a mat to lie on, a drum or mask.

How easily a Health Food Shop can mask
subversive intentions! This salad of words
is better than their greens. Vermilion scarves –
shall I wear those? Brush kohl on my eyes?
Retrieve my soul at the One Heart Centre lodge
in a sundance lead by Leah in peacepaint?

She, part Sioux, mixed snow with her paint
on fieldwork in Bransk, for a shaman's mask.
Victoria B.C. is much too British. I lodge
a complaint against that in my head, find words,
the rudest I can, for begonias. Soon I'm all eyes
for bangles, bandanas and scarves.

A ring of women with a rope of scarves
supports me that week-end. I begin to paint
with glitz and dung, learn to make up my eyes
so that nothing's lacklustre. Mask after mask
falls away: 'Woman', 'White', 'Urban', the words
sing into sense in the Sweat Lodge.

The mother drum beats again in the lodge –
a cedar womb with umbilical scarves.
Now I'm a soundthrough, a per-son whom words
can heal. Yogini songs, the blue, blue paint
decorating a yurt, help me let go of the mask
that has hidden my heart and open my eyes

to shine like headlamps, or the night-time eyes
of beasts, fox, say, or badger which lodge
underground by day. I may decide to mask
my teeth and do the dance of scarves,
a new Salome. Bells and body paint
create a self with no need for words.

Why not get real with a Thru-the-Mask
adventure? Paint lurex eyes, invent words
that lodge and change scars into scarves?

THE KALEIDOSCOPE

I saw it in Afflick's window
on the way to the park,
a black triangular tube.
Afflick, who'd sold me gumdrops,
my rubber Popeye
and set of celluloid dwarfs,
talked of a glass prison –
at least that's what I heard.
I held it to my eye like Nelson
and turned the lens so fast
I couldn't keep up
with the Catherine wheels and stars
shooting out and collapsing
into a shaft of light,
a tunnel of diamond,
the heart of the eye.

It took fourteen weeks to collect
fourteen threepenny bits
in a pillarbox tin.
The last one in was the size
of the knot in my gut –
but Afflick had kept it aside.
I galloped home with my prize,
and wouldn't put it away
with the Spanish dancer doll,
inside the wardrobe; I was a child
who needed to flounce.
I tucked the kaleidoscope
through the belt of my navy mac

and ran into the street
as if I was wearing scarlet.
When it slipped and broke
my mother laughed.

Years on I see the end of the story.
I have her weeping too
for bits of broken glass,
glinting little mirrors on the pavement.
Or I see us weeping for each other.
Could that be true? I need it to be so,
to have her a brilliant dot
and me a prism where
nothing is broken beyond repair,
and there are only patterns
I must look into.

RENT

They teach you what it is to mourn
before the hearse sets off. A woman, terse
as any wardress, beckoned me. Her belt
dividing skirt from shirt was buckled
by steel which she unhinged into a tool
of trade, a razor-blade contraption.

Quite brisk about the measurements required,
like any tailor making alterations,
she said 'I cut, you pull – at least three inches.'
Too tired to disobey, too proud to keep intact
a garment that I cared for, I prepared myself.
But when she had me say, word for word,

the proper blessing, like any clerk of court
swearing a witness in, I blurted out, by rote
'Blessed art thou, O Lord our God,
King of the Universe' ... then paused.
Concisely she performed the rest.

I sensed her scruples went beyond the Law –
she liked her job. My roll-neck ripped apart
left throat exposed and hint of breast.
She said 'Keep this on at least a month –
should be a year,' as if ignorant
of cuts I wear, like any mourner,

not next to the skin, as prescribed,
but incised into a natural zest
that each new death pares off. I minded this,
the razor's edge, the rent paid now.

According to Orthodox Jewish Law, a funeral must take place within 24 hours of a death and next of kin are required to have an item of clothing rent.

HOUSE

I go back to the street where I lived,
and 45 hasn't changed except

steps scrubbed with white pumice stone
are now painted redbrick

and there's a brand new door,
light oak veneer, small glass fan.

The house has let go of a look
that was more direct,

as when blue diamond panes
blazed if the light was on

and I went upstairs to bed
watched by the eyes of God.

THE VISIT

The paintings were even brighter
than we remembered; the familiar angel
with flecks of peacock in his auspicious wings

flared from the wall; gravity of hair
falling like rain, gold halo suns,
and that courteous offer of a lightbulb pear,

all one vast annunciation, whose colours
took hold. And, no, the curator replied,
they had not been recently cleaned.

Memories came flying; I recalled
the way a colleague once appraised me
saying "You are looking very beautiful these days."

I'd paused at the road's edge where car doors
opened like wings, surprised that anyone at all
had noticed such new love, transfiguring.

THE HILL

Opposite the house there's a hill,
a slope of two long fields up to a ridge
which I've watched for seventeen years
from the table. I've seen its neutral soil
passionately redden with poppies
or grass come lilac out of a mist.
I've heard bullocks cry on that hill
before seeing their bulk, the way
they nudge themselves along like boulders.
I've looked up to that hill,
looked up then looked away, to eat or talk
and I've turned my back on it
when the curtains were drawn.
Even a hill shut out exerts a pull –
you sense sky using it as a headrest.
In spring I've walked up a path
glinting with eyebrights and yellowhammers
for the view from a stand of beech.
Land falls away through the trees
into the valley and into that light place
you can't quite name on top of a hill.
This one has held my casual gaze
like the coin from a Roman soldier's pocket
which has just been uncovered.
It's only since leaving the house I realise
that the best view has always been
from indoors, from window panes
squared like a grid to draw by.
I've seen the authority of fog
wiping out cattle, trees, grass, everything,
and then the hill come through again
like the idea of help.

MARGARET'S HOUSE

She went through a door in a wall
and from the end of a very long path
saw a house standing there
like houses that children draw –

blue paintwork against white stone,
square windows, a middling door
and an enclosed garden. This place,
you'd not imagine outside the wall,

was the presence that children know
is always there, although
a garden may be wild
and apple trees too tall.

The house had four main rooms;
she chose to live inside
that first view. Later there'd be
windows with small panes

and, seen from upstairs, a hill,
a row of trees and roofs
where chalk air turns to sky
and not the black, black smoke

which children draw.

THROUGH A DOOR IN A WALL

When I saw the rampant bushes,
silver, green, dark coppery red
and was amazed by a jumble of flowers

coming and going,
tradition of scent,
rosemary, roses, mint,

there was so much past about
I began to think of roots –
all the transactions that brought

the Siberian iris and Ginko tree
over and under the earth.
I could have been anywhere.

This garden, out of sync. with now,
enclosed a rare sweetness.
I've heard how bees steer to nectar

with retinas that recognise
and then retain landmarks.
When I'm dead someone may detect

from my donated eyeballs
or else my brain lying on a slab
where I was making for and why

I went to extremes
though not far enough.
La petite mort –

isn't that what everyone wants?
Or, to move
out of one's body into everywhere

for longer than minutes?
Suppose, after all, we have souls
but they can't taste and see

won't they mourn the body?
Don't we need the weight
of light filtered through petals

in a garden like this?

THE FROG'S PRINCESS

That night, finding him in my bed,
within kissing distance,
I wanted to take the stare
off his face – those eyes
all bulge and goggle.
Then I saw their depth, a look
that could take me anywhere
backwards in time. I recalled
an aquarium under the sea where
I'd pressed my face to the glass
of a wolf-eel's tank, mesmerised
by a little reptilian head
with eyeballs lifting off
like spaceships that settled
into an expression beyond
a seal-pup's dopey smile
or the pout of fish –
like that of some new-born child
you swear has been here before.
The frog was like him,
but when he gulped and a mouth
smelling of weed or bull-kelp
came close to my lips
I flinched and held out my hand
to stop his jump and touched
a spasm of green, a creature trying
to slither out of himself.
I've been so often trapped
in flesh that didn't feel mine
I wondered what he could see
when he gazed into a pond;
he took my sigh as a signal
to kiss. I loved him best
the moment before he changed,
a small, crouched, alien thing
in need of a body.

FACE-TO-FACE

For Maurice Riordan

If that device for sensing and display
were re-arranged
would it much matter? Imagine
the nose, which keeps eyes
decently spaced,
split down the middle, each half
put in a socket below the brow,
while nostrils flare
where eyes were and the mouth
pours down a cheek.
Suppose eyes were horizontally slit
like a goat's, or clownish,
crossed, patched, trapezoidal –
the nose a rhombus and the mouth
occluded into an ellipse
of litmus paper
that turns red or blue
from fear or anger,
and ranges through all the colours
when pursed for a kiss or an oyster.

Do we need to show our emotions
by a flicker, a gape or a twitch?
Are we built into the skin of our faces
as onion flesh into its sheath?
What if we went down the street
with our faces peeled off
and our bodies racing
towards one another
to come as close as we can
to nerve-endings?

FERRET

"A hob after his jill,"
Rob said of that red ferret
streaking through my house
unexpectedly. Next door,
kept in a hidden pen,
was his albino found
on Eggardon Hill. "Hold her",
he said and put her in my hands.
I felt her white fur shiver.

Later, the village news –
Robbie's jill had escaped,
and he was not there.
I put on gardening gloves,
found her across the road,
cowering under railings,
squinting up
with one red eye appealing
like a stitched wound.

What did the creature want?
A same-species mate, perhaps,
not him, not holes
he thrust her in for scuts.
I knelt to offer a hand
ungloved. She slithered on
as if she smelled nothing,
nothing to be afraid of,
and writhed against my breast.

I stroked her like a cat;
she did not purr
as I did deep inside
retrieving her.

THE CAT WHO IS GAME FOR ANYTHING

Why do I fear her leap
onto the sill of an open window
two storeys high in the house?
She's a well balanced cat
but so eager to catch
whatever disturbs the air
I can't help thinking that
an orange-tip or fly
might make her hurtle
into free fall
like some daft woman
dazzled by despair.

OUT OF SUMMER

A one-toned stuttering note
told me the parent was near
and knew its fledgling caught

in the garden. My cat at the door
greeted me gaping; a wing
had forced open her jaw.

She dropped, skittered, dragged
then let the small bird go.
I saw it flutter – a rag

still trying to be a bird.
The parent could not know
that when I picked up a stone

and struck the infant's head
I wanted to stop its pain.
It cheeped just once and died.

Of course it was just behaviour –
that one shriek in reply when
the garden flew out of summer.

WHITE

It's time for a new dove
so this year I won't buy
camels, kings or angels
or blown tin balls
but scour the shops
for a white bird
to replace the one
grey and moulting now
after seventeen years
from our first row
that blew the gold star
from the tree's top needle.
What did you/I say
beyond repair until
the gift I made to signal
words couldn't drown us?
After more difficult times
again I offer you a dove
as one might renew a vow.
Look, it is soft and white
as innocence and, yes, as arsenic –
a grain of which features in
the complex purity of love.

HALF WAY TO MADRID

Not knowing the size of the earth
Columbus discovered Cuba
which, back in Valladolid,
he described as off-shore from Japan.

Not knowing the size of love
could it be we're mistaken
if we think we've reached our goal
when we're only half way to Madrid?

TAILORS

I think continually of those whose lives
did not quite fit, like my two celibate
uncles in their father's shop,

who when he died, kept up his window,
as a frieze of dated fashion-plates
and bald, brown dummies looking vaguely stumped.

Their hot, back room smelled of chalk and smoke.
I saw them clench their mouths on niggling pins
with such a day-to-day bravura.

Tongue-tied myself and always out of place
among black slabs of cloth, I thought them glum,
though they let me try their long bronze thimbles.

I've moved on, not penny-pinched like them,
but find a remnant of their lives, that hod
around the heart – its dark, its weight

that could be fire, as obstinate and slow
as tailors who cut and pressed, whose own live coals
blazed to give flat irons steam to go.

FURTHER ON

The view was not featureless
as we thought on arrival
when the eye found no rest

on a sea whose colour
was unstoppable, without
mountains, lighthouse, harbour

to focus vision. When the heat
abated, a wind blew up
curdling the sea to white

and islands on the horizon
emerged. True, they vanished
in next day's mist and again

our gaze was emptied;
but weren't the sea's brilliancies
enough? What did we need

beyond blue and aquamarine,
the shimmer of tiles or enamel?
Something plain

and hard-edged would do,
beyond the infinitely moving,
to put a stop to our looking.

"WHEN EPIPHANY OCCURRED AND YOU MET THE GOD"

I was somewhere else, I was
something else, I began
to run like a horse
round the stadium at Delphi
empty at twilight;
I was on a mountain when
a stone leapt out of scree
into its selfhood of light
and I saw the diamond of diamonds
until, in an instant, it died back
into mica and gravel;
and, of all places,
I was in Waitrose store when
onions revealed themselves
in a moment more than itself,
a moment that took the shape
of cupolas and domes,
the rotund architecture
of Byzantium.
Of course I peel and weep
like everyone but when
the epiphany of the god occurred
there was a hole
as large as life inside and
it was flooded with the joy
of perceiving –
can you call it that – when
there is no perceiver there
only the eye, welling up?

THE EYE-BATH

For John Lucas

Then, the best blue was that of an eye-bath
which mother used to rinse grit or styes.

Now there's sea through a glass of ouzo,
a man is mending a yellow net

and the sun is on it, I watch the way
he slips light over his redbrown fingers.

Yesterday the Meltemi drove
a clear sky all over the harbour.

A boat is moored with round, red rings
as chunky as my grandma's bobbins.

When I was eight the little glass scoop
healed more with its blue than with boracic.

Today there's a sheet of bright blue glass,
something pricks in my eye, I think it's colour.

PHOTOGRAPHER

Two hornets in a thistle, my best still;
best action shot – the mating dance

of male and female albatross
before the crew and I were almost lost

in an Antarctic snow storm.
"Unearthly love", one critic wrote,

seeing birds with wings two metres long
mirror each other's swoop and glide.

I once filmed ads. of yoghurt pots,
a bored and happy man until

I read about our icthyosaurian soul,
the shivering happiness which comes

from nature. I found a knack
of cosying up to macaques and baboons,

their tender, grooming hands,
and won a prize or two.

Ambitious friends advised
go where the action is and show the world

the world that makes the news; they did –
a child on sand, closed eyes, lids sealed

by flies; a face, all ash and scab,
emerging from a burnt out tank.

I stick to meerkats, or the Asian plains
and poppies, in slow motion, opening up.

MONK OF HEMIS, LADAKH

Last week I blessed a girl
who kissed my hand. Her plait
hung down her crimson frock
like a rope. It hauled me down
from prayer to the two round foothills
of her back, to two small pots
as firm as the first apricots I pick
in August. And her toes shone.

Since my return I've developed a cough.
I practise breathing, focus on the throat,
then move to Svadhistana, Vam, Vishnu,
the genital centre in the diagram
a holy man once gave me.
Grief begins in the lungs
this lama said. I have thought
about the suffering in the world
and learned to control my breath.

Today I was rebuked, I dared to say
that our thousand-headed Buddha
should have a thousand penises
to extend compassion.
The thin air of Hemis
begins to weigh on my chest.
I have no desire to be holy –
all desire is a rope,
for my mind moves, this way and that,
through the knots of a sandal,
and a pigtail of black hair I must undo.

She is here in my redbrown room
when the dust comes to life
in the light of an open door.
She is in the shrine room,
in the beat of the drum,
in the spin of the prayer-wheel,
in the bowls of rancid milk.
And she is above the tree line
where goats straggle to find
even a single grass blade.
She has become my foothold,
I have married her with my prayer.

THE COPPER BEECH

It wasn't the sun I watched set, last night,
but the tree in the yard:
the bark and boughs of a copper beech
took on an applegreen skin that thinned
to a membrane of light and burned
orange, gold, red,
as if it had decided to unearth itself
and unlock the sky.

We know how love can transform people
and they shine.
Nothing, no one was loving this copper beech
to such a pitch though I
close-up and clear-eyed saw
how it incandesced then stopped,
went black from head to foot,
as if what had not loved it had quite gone,
and night, inside it, waited to flow out.

FOXGLOVES

They arrest the eye like pylons,
or, like other highnesses, confer
a sense of occasion.
There is such lineage here
it's as if their roots have tapped
the other side of summer
to make that mauvish red
resonate. Dead Man's Bells
some call these spikes
whose top buds, knuckle-pale,
stay clenched whilst underneath,
pendulous and pocked inside,
these hollow things unfold
an ambiguous beauty.
They stimulate the heart
before it's stricken.

This year a single stalk
with outsize flower lengths
in triple lines
became an abacus
of living digits.
I counted up a hundred, longed
to try them on for size
or, rather, find again the child
who knows at her finger-tips
how she fits in with summer
the way that bees are part,
confiding each speck of hair
of their whole being
to those corpuscular spots.

BLACKTHORN

I can't remember when we agreed
that the blackthorn this spring
had been better than ever,
or when it was that she said
'What does it mean?
It must mean something.' –
as if every packed twig
were a sign,
like red skies at night,
or the berries she'd count on the holly.

I'm trying to recall
whether it was before or after she spoke
of her son dying,
that we exclaimed about the hedgerows'
intensity of white,
and were not adequate
with words like 'snow' and 'drifts',
and 'dizzying',
and how 'the ground shifts'
when you walk amongst it.

LARVA

I've not gone down on my knees
on a rock in the Himalaya
like the man I met tagging the bees
of South East Asia.

I'd stopped, in the heat, to watch
how he put his ear to a crack
listening for signals, to catch,
in his butterfly net,

feathered hairs tipped with pollen,
or bees, in pairs, spinning
in copulation or the swollen
ovipositors of a queen.

I thought a life could go by
without kneeling down to inspect
an insect's shins and thighs,
to know a different species

by its body-parts.
Then, this summer, I gazed
at a creature caught by the cat.
Not worm or snake

but a smooth, segmented body
reared up, on my hand, and I saw
how light came through its amber belly
and made it pearly as if

this crawling insect had a soul
not visible in egg or pupa,
nor even in the Death's Head imago
which enters any hive for honey.

SNAILING

The field was a tip;
stalks, cans, hens,
a collapsed old coop
all a monochrome brown
where the dun-coloured snails
were invisible to me.
An old man in a sailor's cap
talked to his three ginger cats
following the trail of his stick.
Each time he stooped I bent too;
he scooped up snails
but I only found pebbles.
Then stones in the rubbly wall,
a dull breadcrust colour,
made themselves known
as pink, green and purple,
blooming in the year's first rain
that sent the molluscs.
A woman bundled in black
showed me her sackful, unloosed
Greek excitement, pointed
to coiled leaves and seed-heads
and I joined in at last,
collecting fat shells glued
in twos and threes by flesh
tacky as used chewing gum.
A single compact snail, raring to go
put out its horns in a decisive V.

SNOW GLOBE

Remember how you'd turn one upside down?
Sleight of hand or something in the dome
made him and her disappear
over and over. A storm
would wipe them out, they'd reappear,
and grin like garden gnomes,
not beautiful, not precarious either,
when you stopped shaking.

I'd like one now, six feet tall,
clear glass covering real people,
and strength enough to pitch the thing about,
to flurry them. But they'd be reassured
that they, the snow and I are just a game
of make-believe. This power
to make them come and go
is child's play, and no,
I never meant to shake too hard
my first cold globe that fell
out of the palm of my hand,
and from safe keeping.

HOMING IN

I walk out
to the edge of my mind
where there's a line
between two countries
as when I stood in an ocean
on that parallel where
American and Canadian waters
meet in one rippling wave.

I am trying to find
where the dead may be
and whether the brain
has made the correct
cartographic decision
or whether it's only –
the brain I mean –
something you whirr against
and break, like a butterfly
losing aerial precision
when trapped indoors
and fazed by glass.

I've heard the monarch kind
travel thousands of miles
across seas and mountains
via milkweed trails.
Are we digitalised
for homing in
on that dark place
where the dead are hidden?

There is no evidence for this
no evidence at all except
sometimes I walk
to the edge of my mind
waving my passport.

CACTUS

She lay on the hospital bed
like a trussed-up hen, dangling
one leg down; the other stretched
wishbone thin from a rucked nightie.
Was she asleep, so untucked in?
And should I wait? Suppose she woke?
Last week she'd called her son
a money-grubbing fart, and made him weep,
so not-herself and so percipient.
He'd said 'She'll not come back,
she'll vegetate.' She'd been my neighbour.

Well, let her be a cabbage, plump,
with leaves so firm and tight
slugs couldn't get at her heart;
or, a horse-mushroom, beaming
like a headlight. I looked away;
hairs stood out on her chin like spikes.
If she were a cactus she'd survive
like prickly pears or succulents
reduced to hairs and wax, to stems
that open up at night to breathe,
and peak with vivid, soft florets.

Let her accomplish death like that.

THE GAME

My painted doll from Russia
had a waist fitted into hips
as if you couldn't split
the body in two
when in fact you could –

eight or nine times
for eight or nine women
who would roll in halves,
hands severed and missing
their rightful arms

until you sorted out the size
of head, the coloured sleeves
and each doll whole again was made
to nestle inside another one
in a losing- and-finding- mother game.

Babushka, bubbah, momma, mam,
these were some of the names I gave
to that wooden peasant
whose headscarf covered
a pleasant Latvian face.

You might undo her many times
before you came to the motherling
whom you couldn't divide,
who was solid right through
but tiny, tiny
and easily lost when put aside.

GLASSES

Once she had frames
pink, perspex, winged
that uplifted her gaze.
I saw her eyes shrinking
behind pebbled specs
and a child disappear
in the magnified rage
of someone who wanted to read
the whole world and who needed
the world's abundance of sand,
rock crystal, chalcedony, quartz,
all of its silica heated
to go into lenses like those
Spinoza was grinding
when he saw facets of God.

Now through bifocals I peer
at my mother, her wedding
where she dwindles in tulle
to a mermaid's swish tail
down the synagogue steps.
Look, she is almost unbalanced
by a huge mock-orange bouquet,
but father, wearing white gloves,
is beaming, holding her arm.
Her face is quite naked
and eyes contradict
the smile-shape of her lips
as if the camera caught her
wincing, as if the camera knew
of the needle which slipped
into the sole of her foot
when she was stitching her veil.

SKINS

On holiday I see five skins
hang from an olive tree near the beach.
They're headless but have cloven feet
where a sure-footedness still clings.
They are long, thin goats, flayed
not alive, like Marsyas,
or that murdered aborigine
whose skin was peeled for tribal scars
and sent with his smoked head
to be displayed in England.
I'm jolted from my ouzo mood
by pelts tense as some memories–
'the kid my father bought for two zuzim'
in the Passover ballad –*There was a fire
that ate the stick that beat the dog etc.
till the Angel of Death himself came down.*
I can't recall what happened next.
My father called my aunt 'our kid';
none of us knew where or when
our forebears last kept goats.
They died in so many different places
I can't begin even to trace their names,
but recognise their outlines
on the tree of life like skins
to be cured in the sun,
I wear the same strong markings.

FIRST NATION MASKS

Nothing to do with me –
the cannibal bird, beak

bright blue, the goggle eye.
I can't put on the bear's

sad head, the muzzle
of a double-barrelled nose,

blind eyeholes. But suppose
I have a near death encounter

in the sea, swim to land,
live at the forest's edge

half-mad, feed on salal berries
and put spikes through my lips

will I then earn the right
to wear the mask of animal?

Even now might an original man
teach me to dance?

MASK

Stone head in Vancouver,
eyes closed, doesn't miss

his other half in Paris
whose eyes are open.

Asleep or dead, stone head
in Vancouver doesn't ache

because his head is split
like a walnut.

I envy this old mask
his own glass case

in which he can survive
a missing face.

HAZEL NUTS

Late August, pale and premature,
some lay in ruts below the hedge,
nestled in twin green bracts.
Rain or birds, the snap of twigs
had made them drop. Others ripened.
I found one sliced across the top
like a breakfast egg. I put it by –
a globe with a black hole inside.

Julian held in the palm of her hand
an item like a hazel nut,
and saw the whole world made and kept
forever. Only a mind in love
can see like that. I took leave
of my senses once, a nut-case
in a truckle bed. I keep it by –
this husk scooped clean.

Trouvaille or a trivial thing?
The more that I look into it
the more I see a hole
I can't see round. I'm perplexed;
my mind is more or less intact
but only a shell unless I find
a seed shaped like a globe inside
that nothing cracks.

Julian of Norwich, anchoress and mystic, 1342 – some time after 1416.

DANÄE COMPARES NOTES WITH EUROPA

She rolled her eyes as cattle do,
when I told her the god
entered my eight openings
as sheer light, how desire,
mine, shaped the form
of his gold descent.
Her eyes looked horizontally
slit, like those of cattle seeing
a blur advance, the tip
of danger. She said the god
bore her away gently,
then she was tossed and gored
but no, not raped,
and she challenged my delight –
had I heard the roar of gold
or been overpowered by the smell
of spittle and dung?
We shook with laughter
at stories we'd tell to make claims
for our future children,
my son, who with mirror-light
would kill a monster;
her divided boy,
who would people a continent.

THE BACK-YARD TREE

If I should see again the tree
whose name I still don't know, whose white
astonished me when flowers broke
out of black and from the back-yard step
I saw our air-raid shelter newly lit
by the overhang's flare
and didn't know what to do except
invite Annie, Peter and Joe
across the street to come and pick –
in fact we stripped the whole tree bare
without a thought of damage done –
if that first tree should re-appear,
now I can't knock on doors
for children, I might wait nearby
holding myself like an empty jam-jar.

THE BUZZARD

lifts off, a Tiger Moth with eyes
on its underwings
that can possibly hypnotise
a stoat pursuing
a rabbit; do these eyes add
power? This bird will soar,
having hunted and fed,
sheerly for pleasure.
Yet what does it mean
by a kittenish mewl
out of keeping with its grand design
of built-to-kill?
Is it a mechanical prayer to heavens
which also prey, with bigger talons?

CURTAINS

She means to put curtains up
now it's past high summer.
She says she doesn't want the dark
looking in. Me? I'd keep night
as close as I can to where I sit, seeing
at nightfall the attentive stance
of plants in the garden, how roses quieten
and there's a frisson of marguerites
while the overgrown appletrees
look heavy with fruit
where blackness fills
the space between branches.

ERYNGIUM

Having seen its globe
giving off a blurred light
blue as the adonis butterfly,
and, underneath, a serrature
of leaves shaped into stars,
and the way silverblue bleeds
into the stem, I can grasp
why the design of this plant
dominates any bed. At a glance
you see that, like teasels,
it's not to be touched, though bees
squat on its spiny tufts
not minding the absence of hearts
to dive into. It's too sharp
for a child to use as a clock;
the whole flower's a gadget
some might gauge their love by –
it is more accurate than daisies

FRESCOES
(UMBRIA, SPOLETO)

The walls appeal – those conical breasts
of women offered to Christ-bambini,
and angels swinging with great cheerfulness.

They corner most scenes. Naive wings
worn formally as extra limbs
make you believe in them as facts

you wish could happen now; until that Pietà
and that small angel witnessing, who acts
quite humanly, lifts both hands to his head,

warding off an agonising sound.
You almost hear the long drawn-out Christ,
and feel his white pelt weighing down

the woman's accurate lap. You realise
the helplessness of angels, and that your own
full-grown frightened hands are fluttering

like nervous wings. Should they go or stay?
Bring cups of tea or wipe the sweat away?
Or turn the volume down?

BLWD. MONTMARTRE: AFTER PISSARRO

Angling in the rain he caught the light,
set it in gas lamps, then left the scene,
like one whose work it was to change the dark
with stick and lantern.
This night invites you in;
a lamp-post at the road's edge bars your way.
What happens next is almost unresolved,
a cab has broken rank, lights in a row
float towards the vanishing point.
One pavement is awash with orange red,
and there are luminous blue walls
with small, pale awnings where
lovers meet in bars or shops.
Except there are no people here,
only a crowd of brush-strokes broken
to look like them, shadowy
as men and women sometimes are at night,
without the touch of flesh
that lights them up.

MINOANS

Swallows have nested
behind the frescoes

and between palace columns
wings are whirring

as if the birds are
words in action

which broken pencils
loop and loop

now there's nothing to do
since the roof has fallen.

The constant movement,
the constant twitter

from sticks
and eggshell thin foundations

signal high art. The imperious young
open their beaks, soon they'll learn

their aerobatic swoop
over the bull's cracked horn

where thin-waisted acrobats
are doing their handstands

IN MY AUNT'S BEDROOM

When we open her wardrobe door
we can hear

an animal presence breathe
and our fingers tingle

as hands run down the shine
of mink or beaver.

A nephew buries a face
in the coats she wore.

There isn't a river smell
or line of blood,

no yelp of cubs bereft
in snowland

only the weight of pelts,
silver fox, sable,

a casual, musquaw jacket.
They look so small left hanging

without a swagger in them –
her dream of men with guns

bringing her their skins

THUJA TREE

I think its green might go on
forever, like a landscape

I once saw from a train, three days
of cloud, rain, and conifers droning on,

one note of high-pitched green
that nothing could get through, although

I hoped a bear or a moose might burst out
from all that cover

to stop my being bored.
So I kept looking and began to see

how those trees stretch themselves and swirl
even when standing still, voracious for light.

People frown at the height of our Thuja,
saying "Why don't you cut it down?"

seeing only an enemy of sun
with no more significance for sky

than to be an opening giant umbrella
making shade, taking too much from soil,

standing in the way of what might grow
or a view you might choose.

Yet there are views that choose you
only through a dark presence

like the moon I saw this August
caught in the Thuja's branches

boring its way through,
a wolf-moon, fiercely alive.

POLLARD

The scuttle of squirrels dislodged
shows how little I know
about nests. Is it a hole
that they miss, or runways
into the sky? My poplar is lopped,
has three stumps and a head
that grins like a gargoyle.
These are the aspects of loss –
a manikin's arms and one leg,
stark and jaunty, kicking high.
There's pent up energy in bark
stripped of branch, twig, sprout,
shaved of all blur.
And yes, I might prefer
this torso except that I fear
that this year the tree may be dead
and stand in the way of Spring
awkwardly, like grief held in.
This pollard is meant to reach out
with fingers like wands,
to hold up a head that is crowned,
to shelter small birds.

NO TIME TO REFLECT

Sometimes they wanted to walk away
from the noise, the phones, the clack
of heels on floors to and from
the coffee machines, the stress
of the floors, the flash of screens
endlessly changing their zeros
and the sly arrival of faxes.
Sometimes they wanted to get away
from all that, take a walk, perhaps,
over the bridge slung like a hammock
between wharves and the Heights.
But, constructed of steel, glass,
pipes, arteries, ducts,
wired up with a mesh of nerves
like the brain's own plumbing,
they could not move although
one can imagine, at times, they felt
the buzz of power getting them down,
as well as their everyday elation
when, heads in the clouds,
sky was the limit.

That fine September day,
when like cats on a doorstep
their people sniffed
woodsmoke and apples,
vestige of autumn even in cities,
they had no time to reflect
the shape of nosedive and flames.
They gaped, gasped, shook
erupted into an attack
of coughing, so loud
nothing could be heard
but the clatter of ribs
coming apart, and the spill

of brains and groins.
They lay in their stone's dust
knowing as much or as little
as metal scraps of planes
why it is men grow tall
and the extent of clay.

THE CULTIVATOR OF SILKWORMS QUESTIONS THE ORACLE

Will my silkworms be fruitful
this year, if there's drought?
Does the size of their horns
show their strength? How long
must I be absent from Cos?
Should my wife and our sons
depart for the mainland?
When can they sail?

Who's my main rival?
Will he cut prices?
Which spy advised him
of last year's fourth moult?
Should I sell all my stock,
or keep the best fibre?
Does the smell of raw silk
give my wife pleasure?

Is it true that my wife
has made up a potion
from one grain of eggs
pickled in wine?
Will my neighbour find out
I've killed some of his goats?
Which slave will watch over
my mulberry trees?

If a worm shakes its head
for three days only
how can it eject
a thread a mile long?
Does a blood-red moon
affect the moths' laying?
Will the girls have warm breasts
to hold the cocoons?

My wife is now pregnant —
has she been faithful?
Will she bear me a daughter?
What makes spinning-glands grow?
Why is it some horns
emit no hard liquid?
Shall I end up a pauper?
Is her love for me dead?

OTHER BOOKS FROM SHOESTRING PRESS

MORRIS PAPERS: Poems Arnold Rattenbury. Includes 5 colour illustrations of Morris's wallpaper designs. "The intellectual quality is apparent in his quirky wit and the skilful craftsmanship with which, for example, he uses rhyme, always its master, never its servant." *Poetry Nation Review.*

ISBN 1 899549 03 X   £4.95

INSIDE OUTSIDE: NEW AND SELECTED POEMS Barry Cole. "A fine poet ... the real thing." *Stand.*

ISBN 1 899549 11 0   £6.95

COLLECTED POEMS Ian Fletcher. With Introduction by Peter Porter. Fletcher's work is that of "a virtuoso", as Porter remarks, a poet in love with "the voluptuousness of language" who is also a master technician.

ISBN 1 899549 22 6   £8.95

STONELAND HARVEST: NEW AND SELECTED POEMS Dimitris Tsaloumas. This generous selection brings together poems from all periods of Tsaloumas's life and makes available for the first time to a UK readership the work of this major Greek-Australian poet.

ISBN 1 8995549 35 8   £8.00

ODES Andreas Kalvos. Translated into English by George Dandoulakis. The first English version of the work of a poet who is in some respects the equal of his contemporary, Greece's national poet, Solomos.

ISBN 1 899549 21 8   £9.95

LANDSCAPES FROM THE ORIGIN AND THE WANDERING OF YK Lydia Stephanou. Translated into English by Philip Ramp. This famous book-length poem by one of Greece's leading poets was first published in Greece in 1965. A second edition appeared in 1990.

ISBN 1 899549 20 X   £8.95

POEMS Manolis Anagnostakis. Translated into English by Philip Ramp. A wide-ranging selection from a poet who is generally regarded as one of Greece's most important living poets and who in 1985 won the Greek State Prize for Poetry.

ISBN 1 899549 19 6   £8.95

THE FREE BESIEGED AND OTHER POEMS Dionysios Solomos
In English versions. Edited by Peter Mackridge.

ISBN 1 899549 41 2   £8.00

SELECTED POEMS Tassos Denegris. Translated into English by Philip Ramp. A generous selection of the work of a Greek poet with an international reputation. Denegris's poetry has been translated into most major European languages and he has read across the world.

ISBN 1 899549 45 9   £6.95

THE FIRST DEATH Dimitris Lyacos. Translated into English by Shorsha Sullivan. With six masks by Friedrich Unegg. Praised by the Italian critic Bruno Rosada for "the casting of emotion into an analytical structure and its distillation into a means of communication", Lyacos's work has already made a significant impact across Europe, where it has been performed in a number of major cities.

ISBN 1 899549 42 0   £6.95

A COLD SPELL Angela Leighton. "Outstanding among the excellent", Anne Stevenson, *Other Poetry*.

ISBN 1 899549 40 4   £6.95

BEYOND THE BITTER WIND: Poems 1982–2000, Christopher Southgate.

ISBN 1 899549 47 1   £8.00

SEVERN BRIDGE: NEW & SELECTED POEMS, Barbara Hardy.

ISBN 1 899549 54 4   £7.50

WISING UP, DRESSING DOWN: POEMS, Edward Mackinnon.

ISBN 1 899549 66 8   £6.95

CRAEFT: POEMS FROM THE ANGLO-SAXON Translated and with Introduction and notes by Graham Holderness. Poetry Book Society Recommendation.

ISBN 1 899549 67 6   £7.50

TESTIMONIES: NEW AND SELECTED POEMS Philip Callow. With Introduction by Stanley Middleton. A generous selection which brings together work from all periods of the career of this acclaimed novelist, poet and biographer.

ISBN 1 899549 44 7   £8.95

PASSAGE FROM HOME: A MEMOIR Philip Callow. Angela Carter described Callow's writing as possessing "a clean lift as if the words had not been used before, never without its own nervous energy."

ISBN 1 899549 65 X   £6.95

Shoestring Press also publish Philip Callow's novel, BLACK RAINBOW.

ISBN 1 899549 33 1   £6.99

For full catalogue write to:
Shoestring Press
19 Devonshire Avenue
Beeston, Nottingham, NG9 1BS UK
or visit us on www.shoestringpress.co.uk